PENGUIN
SELF-
STARTERS

THE FIVE-HOUR KEYBOARDING COURSE

Madeleine Brearley was born in London in 1958. In 1962 her parents emigrated to Australia and she started school there, but returned two years later when her family decided to settle in Dorset. She was educated at Christchurch Grammar School, Brockenhurst College and Bournemouth College of Technology.

Before graduating in Developmental Psychology from Sussex University, Madeleine Brearley worked as a secretary in London, returning in 1982 to work in television. She is now a freelance television researcher working in children's television. Her writing interests include writing television plays for children, adapting novels and writing short stories.

SERIES EDITORS: Stephen Coote and Brian Loughrey

MADELEINE
BREARLEY •

THE
FIVE-HOUR
KEYBOARDING
COURSE

PENGUIN
BOOKS

PENGUIN BOOKS

Published by the Penguin Group
27 Wrights Lane, London W8 5TZ, England
Viking Penguin Inc., 40 West 23rd Street, New York, New York 10010, USA
Penguin Books Australia Ltd, Ringwood, Victoria, Australia
Penguin Books Canada Ltd, 2801 John Street, Markham, Ontario, Canada L3R 1B4
Penguin Books (NZ) Ltd, 182–190 Wairau Road, Auckland 10, New Zealand

Penguin Books Ltd, Registered Offices: Harmondsworth, Middlesex, England

First published 1987
10 9 8 7 6 5 4 3 2

Printed and bound in Great Britain by
Cox & Wyman Ltd, Reading
Typeset in 10/11½ Linotron 202 Univers Medium.

CONTENTS

INTRODUCTION

Blast! There must be something wrong with this machine. Why don't I get on with typewriters like other people do? One minute I'm doing OK, the next I've typed a line of something that looks like Polish poetry.

The typewriter has been with us for many years. Little did Henry Mill realize in 1714 when he took out a patent on his contraption for the transcribing of letters, that is, the first typewriter, how many hours of frustration, desperation and perspiration he would ensure for those of us grappling with 'the keyboard'.

Whether you type on a wonky old portable manual in the kitchen or operate a computer keyboard with a memory that surpasses that of all living (and dead) elephants, to be able to control it with ease and confidence may still be a dream that eludes many of us for many years!!

This book is aimed at demolishing the myth that one must be born with a typewriter in one's pram or genes pre-programmed for computer input dexterity in order to accomplish keyboard control. Day by day and stage by stage, within a period of five hours (split into ten simple sessions), it will be possible to operate a keyboard with competence. Technique, style, tricks of the trade, typists' tips are outlined step by step and will enable the grappler to become a proficient keyboard user and help to eradicate that amateurish look from the finished article.

Most 'typing-made-ever-so-easy' books are not simple to understand at all! But this one has been tried, tested and passed as a quick and easy way to learn to type and control a keyboard.

WHY SHOULD I BOTHER TO LEARN – IT'S NOT MY REAL JOB

The following is a familiar statement in schools, offices, at parties, during pub chats and wine bar chin-wags. '. . . I've been typing with two fingers for umpteen years, I'm as fast as any trained typist . . .' Then, the speaker admits that when it comes to figures, or having to look at three or four different things all at once, he or she forgets where they are, and fingers start to fall over each other rushing for the wrong keys.

Two-finger typists can and often do reach speeds of more than fifty words per minute – a respectable speed, but the touch typist on an electronic machine can easily surpass 90 wpm. But is it necessary? Yes, of course it is, otherwise nobody would ever bother to learn at all, and in time it would become an ancient art, like using an abacus! It is a fact that more people can type today than ever before and even more want to, but can't.

So why can some people do it and why do others desperately want to? Keyboard control (touch typing) leads to faster typing speeds, but it also has other benefits: **(1)** accuracy; **(2)** superior quality of presentation; and **(3)** it enables the typist to 'copy type', or to read from one document and to type another, without looking at the keyboard. These points might be put to use while typing up hand-written work, computer programming, or even operating a manual typewriter in the dark!

Certain tips and techniques will enable the aspiring home typist to give a professional look to their work and help them to avoid amateur pitfalls that detract from the appearance of a letter, cv, application form, document etc. Remember, if something is badly typed, no matter what it says, it's difficult to award it any importance or authority.

• HOW DOES THIS COURSE WORK?

There are three stages to each session:

(1) **Exercise**   a step-by-step outline of your lesson for the day

(2) **Example**   a neat example of the day's lesson, just how yours will look (it may help some people to look at this before attempting the lesson for the day)

(3) **Explanation**   a summary of the rules, the do's and don't's, the 'what for's' covered in the day's lesson

All you need to have is a keyboard and the three Rs (reading, writing and arithmetic). And this book will give you the three easy Es: the easy exercise, the easy example and the easy explanation.

• HOW LONG DOES THE COURSE TAKE?

It uses a simple system of two days on the course, and one day off, over a period of fourteen days. You should finish the ten-session course in fourteen days. Each session takes 20–30 minutes to complete.

Alternatively, the highly motivated, or those with little spare time, may wish to 'crash' the course and complete it in two days. Sessions 1–5 may be completed in two and a half hours on the first day; the remaining five sessions may be completed in two and a half hours the next day. Dare I suggest that the extremely keen could perhaps undertake the entire course in a single day? Five sessions in the morning and five in the afternoon.

THE BASICS

There is no need to type on your keyboard yet, just glance at it while reading the following:

When touch typing all eight fingers are used with more or less equal regularity. The right thumb is used solely for putting in the space between each word. The left thumb is never used — it waits, poised and ever hopeful!

• THE FIRST RULE

Every single key on the keyboard is operated by a specific finger, the same finger every single time that the key is used. Typing is a strict division of labour and no finger helps out another if it should be stuck elsewhere on the keyboard. So, the letter 'P' is always typed by the same finger, no matter what word it is being typed in. This rule applies for every number and letter, whether small or capital, whether it is an upper- or lower-case letter or character.

• THE SECOND RULE

Each hand has a 'pivot point', that is, a starting position on the keyboard from which it never strays.

The little finger on the left hand is always on the letter 'A' and very rarely moves away from this position. The little finger on the right hand lives on the semi-colon key ';' and, similarly, very rarely moves away from this position. In this manner, each hand is 'pivoted' to a section of the keyboard, with the other fingers stretching out to reach their own keys.

● THE THIRD RULE

While typing, or operating a keyboard, never move your hand away from the keyboard, or more importantly, never remove your little fingers from their pivot points. In the event of their being used to type their own few keys, then and only then, the first finger of the relevant hand temporarily becomes the pivot point.

Gently rest your finger tips on the home keys but don't rest your wrist or the palms of your hands on any part of the keyboard – believe me it makes keyboard control uncomfortable. And that happens to be one of the reasons why some people never progress from their first keyboard lesson – it hurts, and so does wearing your wellington boots on the wrong feet!

● SO WHERE DO THE REST OF MY FINGERS GO?

You may now get out your typewriter/keyboard, flex those finger muscles and carry out the following instructions:

Place the four fingers of your LEFT hand on these keys:

A S D F

These are the 'home keys' of the left hand. Remember that 'A' is the little finger's 'pivot point'.
The fingers resting on these keys are named as follows:

Liv Liii Lii Li
(See diagram p. 18)

Place the four fingers of your RIGHT hand on these keys:

J K L ;

These are the 'home keys' of the right hand.
Remember that the semi-colon key is the little finger's 'pivot point'. Similarly, these fingers are named as follows:

Ri Rii Riii Riv
(See diagram p. 19)

THE KEYBOARD LAYOUT

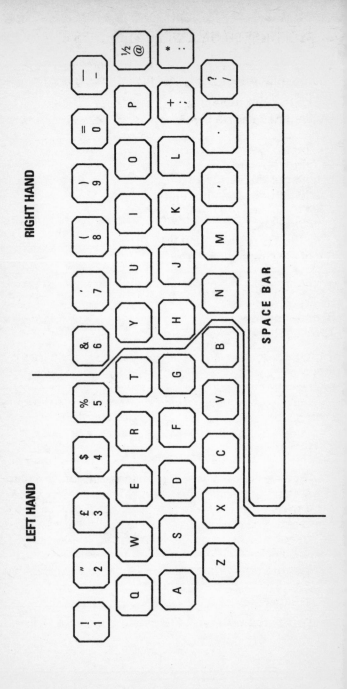

16

• WHICH ONE DOES WHAT?

Do not type anything – just feel the keys belonging to and operated by each finger. Starting with the little finger on the left hand (Liv):

Liv finger operates: **1 q a z** (and the shift key)
Liii finger operates: **2 w s x**
Lii finger operates: **3 e d c**
Li finger operates: **4 5 r f v b g t**
The left thumb does nothing!

Starting with the little finger on the right hand (Riv) feel the following:

Riv finger operates: **0 p ; / : ½ -** (and the shift key)
Riii finger operates: **9 o l .**
Rii finger operates: **8 i k ,**
Ri finger operates: **6 7 u j m n h y**
The right thumb operates the space bar.

As you will soon find out, some fingers are busier than others – that's life! Some keyboards may be set out slightly differently on the extreme right-hand side of the keyboard – don't worry, all these keys are still operated by the little finger of the right hand.

• LEFT HAND EXERCISE

○ Rest the little finger of your left hand on the pivot key: remember, this is the 'A' key. Now place the Liii, Lii and Li fingers on their home keys, the 'S', 'D' and 'F' keys. This should feel comfortable. You may need to adjust the height of your chair, how close you are to the keyboard and so on. The best guide is to be sat with your arms forming right angles at the elbows; the natural length of your arms will determine the distance between you and the keyboard.

○ Stretch out with the Li finger and touch the 'T' key.

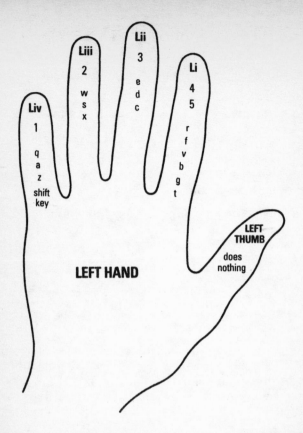

Liv 1 q a z shift key

Liii 2 w s x

Lii 3 e d c

Li 4 5 r f v b g t

LEFT THUMB does nothing

LEFT HAND

○ With the same finger touch the 'F', 'R' and 'V' keys. Do not attempt to type the letters yet, just get the feel of where they are on the keyboard.

○ With the same finger reach for the 'G' and then the 'B' keys. This is going to be one of your busy fingers! You may move your hand as a whole to reach for 'G' and 'B' comfortably by just letting the Lii and Liii move slightly off their own home keys, but whatever you do, keep the little finger on the 'A' key.

○ Finally, feel for the '4' and '5' keys. Again you may need to raise the Lii and Liii fingers off their home keys for this movement, but be sure to keep the little finger firmly on the 'A' key.

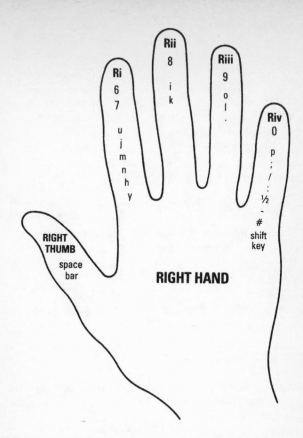

Ri
6
7

u
j
m
n
h
y

Rii
8

i

k

Riii
9

o
l
.

Riv
0

p
;
/
:
½
-
#
shift
key

RIGHT
THUMB

space
bar

RIGHT HAND

○ Now move the Li finger back to its proper place, its own home key, the 'F' key.

○ Everything should now be safely back in place. See where you have been.

○ Explore these keys one more time with your Li finger, so that you get used to the feel of the different stretches to the different keys.

○ Now, with the Lii finger, feel for the 'E', 'D', 'C' and '3' keys. Repeat these movements a few times.

○ With the Liii finger feel for the 'W', 'X', 'S' and '2' keys. You may need to lift Li and Lii off their home keys by half a centimetre or so, but make sure that your little finger sticks to the 'A' key no matter what. Then, bring all four fingers back to their home keys.

○ With the Liv finger feel the 'Q', 'A', 'Z' and '1' keys (remember, while you are using this finger, the Li finger remains firmly attached to the 'F' key and does not move while the little finger is doing its own exploring; temporarily the Li finger acts as a pivot finger). Again, Lii and Liii may need to move off their keys to make typing with the little finger comfortable; leave them in mid-air until the little finger is ready to return to its own home key.

That then is the left hand fully stretched and explored. Each finger is responsible for a small area of the keyboard. Pivoting the hand to a single key enables easy location of each of those areas. All fingers operate several keys, but each key is operated by the one and only finger responsible for it and no other, ever!

When you are ready, read on and explore the keyboard with your right hand.

● RIGHT HAND EXERCISE

○ Rest the little finger of your right hand on the pivot key; don't forget that this is the semi-colon key. Now place Riii, Rii and Ri fingers on their home keys, the 'L', 'K' and 'J' keys. Make sure this feels comfortable.

○ Stretch out with the Ri finger and touch the 'U' and 'M' keys.

○ Now reach for the 'N', 'H' and 'Y' keys. As with the left hand, you may need to let go of the two middle home keys. Raise the Rii and Riii fingers off their own home keys, the 'K' and 'L' keys, in order to allow the Ri finger an easier reach to its furthest keys, but whatever you do, do not remove your little finger from the semi-colon key. This is your right hand pivot point and it is essential not to let go of it unless the little finger is typing one of its other keys, otherwise you will not be able to locate the other home keys with ease.

○ Repeat these feeling and stretching movements a few times. Don't forget it's only typing so don't overdo it and get puffed out!

○ Now with the same finger, the Ri finger, reach for the '6' and '7' keys, again keeping your little finger firmly placed on the semi-colon key.

○ Return all four fingers to their home keys.

○ With the Ri finger on its home key, let your Rii finger feel for the 'I', 'K' and '8' keys. Finally, feel for the comma key on the bottom line.

○ Next, with the Riii finger feel for the 'O', 'L' and '9' keys. Now feel for the full stop key. You may feel the need to lift the Riv finger off its home key and you may do so, as long as the Ri finger stays firmly placed on the 'J' key and in this way temporarily acts as a pivot point.

○ After each stretch has been completed return all four fingers to their home keys.

○ With the Ri finger acting as the pivot point on the 'J' key, let your little finger, the Riv finger, feel for the 'P', nought and solidus key. (These keys may vary from one keyboard to another but, whatever character these keys represent, they will still be operated by the little finger of the right hand.)

○ Don't worry if it all feels a bit awkward at first; this is normal and will pass within a few days.

In brief, as long as you have a finger on a pivot key and the other fingers can reach for their keys, then you are doing fine.

You may find the 'Quick Reference' pages that follow useful when you are doing the sessions, but they are not meant to be learnt off by heart. During any learning process you will hit a 'blank spot' and something you knew so well just escapes you and these reference pages are meant for those very moments and nothing more.

● QUICK REFERENCE: LETTERS

Letter operated by finger		Letter operated by finger	
A	Liv	N	Ri
B	Li	O	Riii
C	Lii	P	Riv
D	Lii	Q	Liv
E	Lii	R	Li
F	Li	S	Liii
G	Li	T	Li
H	Ri	U	Ri
I	Rii	V	Li
J	Ri	W	Liii
K	Rii	X	Liii
L	Riii	Y	Ri
M	Ri	Z	Liv

You may need to refer to this page and the next two pages when you are doing your exercises, but for the moment just glance through them.

● QUICK REFERENCE: NUMBERS AND SIGNS

There may be some variation between different keyboards but, for example, the number 3 will always be typed with the Lii finger, whether or not when you engage the shift key you obtain the £ sign. If there is another character in place of the £ sign, you still use the same finger (Lii) to type it.

Character operated by finger		Character operated by finger	
1 !	Liv	0 =	Riv
2 "	Liii	- __	Riv
3 £	Lii	@ ½	Riv
4 $	Li	; +	Riv
5 %	Li	: *	Riv
6 &	Ri	/ ?	Riv
7 '	Ri	.	Riii
8 (	Rii	,	Rii
9)	Riii	**Space bar**	R thumb

Any keys to the extreme left of your keyboard are typed with the Liv finger and, similarly, any keys on the extreme right of your keyboard are typed with the Riv finger.

● QUICKER REFERENCE

Left hand operates	Right hand operates
A	
B	
C	
D	
E	
F	
G	
	H
	I
	J
	K
	L
	M
	N
	O
	P
Q	
R	
S	
T	
	U
V	
W	
X	
	Y
Z	
1	
2	
3	
4	
5	
	6
	7
	8
	9
	0

● A WORD OF ENCOURAGEMENT

At this point you may feel more confused and mind-boggled than ever before; it's only natural! However, bear the following in mind:

Each key is 'depressed' by the finger nearest to it, and only by the tip of that finger, so you'll find that this means only one finger falls easily on to each key – if it seems awkward it may mean you are using the wrong finger, so check the reference chart. Make sure your little fingers are on their pivot points and that the others are on their home keys, and whenever you have typed a key always return your fingers to their pivot and home keys. (A word of warning: if you don't, nasty mistakes happen – your finger or fingers become disoriented and accidentally hop on to the wrong key, just when you least need or expect it!)

● THE FOURTH RULE

Always return a finger to its home or pivot key after typing a top or bottom row letter/character. (In time this will become automatic.)

● THE FIFTH RULE

Think of each key on the keyboard as a mini trampoline for your finger. Make each finger bounce quickly off the key once it has depressed it and typed its character.

When your fingers are not typing they should be poised just above the keys, hardly touching the keys with their tips.

A PROPER TYPING LESSON

○ Insert some paper into your typewriter/keyboard.

○ Set your margins (it doesn't matter where at this stage).

○ Set your machine to type in single line spacing.

○ Poise your left and right hand over their home keys.

Don't forget 'A' is the pivot key for the left hand little finger.
The semi-colon key is the pivot key for the right hand little
finger. Remember also, the temporary pivot point for the left
hand is Li on the 'F' key. Similarly, the temporary pivot point
for the right hand is the Ri finger on the 'J' key. This allows the
little fingers to dash off and do their bit of typing without losing
your place on the keyboard, and to enable you to type some
of the more stretching keys with the Lii and Liii and Rii and Riii
fingers.

If you think it is going to help you – label your fingers with little
stickers for the first few sessions, so that you can remember
which is Li, Lii, Ri, Rii and so on.

Now read through this session, look at the example, read the
explanation, and come back to this point before doing any
typing.

Type the following words with your left hand three times each.
Keep the right hand ready for action and don't forget to press
the space bar with your right thumb in order to insert the space
between each word.

sad   fed   red   few   ted   get

Now, type the following words with your right hand three times each. Although you won't need to use your left hand, keep it on the keyboard just to get used to the feel of it being there.

kim jim pill mum hun kop

Do make sure you are using the correct fingers. Check with the reference charts. It is better to be very slow but absolutely accurate at this stage. At the end of each word replace all your fingers on their home keys. Don't be afraid to stretch for the necessary keys and to lift off your non-typing fingers to make it easier and more comfortable, but do not remove the little fingers from their keys, unless you are typing another character with these little fingers. When you do, remember that the first finger will become a temporary pivot finger, either on the 'F' key for the left hand, or on the 'J' key for the right hand.

● EXAMPLE

Left hand words   Right hand words

sad sad sad   kim kim kim

fed fed fed   jim jim jim

red red red   pill pill pill

few few few   mum mum mum

ted ted ted   hun hun hun

get get get   kop kop kop

• EXPLANATION

No matter how long it takes, make sure that you do this first exercise with the correct fingers. Check against the keyboard chart. Remember, it takes longer to unlearn mistakes than it does to check the finger chart whenever you are in doubt about your fingering.

Do not attempt to correct any errors yet. (This is a very time-consuming process, especially at the beginning and it will be dealt with in a later section of this book.)

Each successive attempt at the exercises will serve as a mark of your progress and over a period of a few days you will notice some improvement.

Soon, you will know exactly where some of the letters are and, what is more, have no hesitation in knowing which finger to use to type them with. Other keys (and each person is different) will take longer and strangely enough there may be one or two letters that just evade recollection of where they are for ages. Persist – this won't last forever.

At this point in the series of lessons, it may be that your touch-typing speed is nowhere near your two-fingered efforts. Do not let this dissuade you from continuing. Soon you will over-take that old two-fingered speed of yours. For the drivers amongst you, bear in mind that it is possible to drive at 20mph in second gear, but once you have mastered third and fourth gear, your previous speed will appear less than sufficient! Likewise keyboard control with all your fingers!!

THE ALPHABET

With each session, read the lesson, look at the example and read the explanation.

o Insert some paper into your machine and set the margins so that the left one is slightly wider than the right one.

o Now warm up by typing the following words in single line spacing three times each. Although they are left hand only words, keep the right hand on the keyboard as if you were using both hands.

fred   deaf   seed   great   sweet   beggar

o Type the following right hand only words three times each in single line spacing. Keep the left hand on the keyboard just as if you were typing with both hands.

jimmy   lolly   poppy   hum   nim   jumpy

o Don't forget that for both sets of words the space in between each word is made by depressing the space bar with the right thumb.

o Now type the alphabet, slowly, with no spaces between each letter.

o Next, type the alphabet, very slowly, this time with a space between each letter.

o Look at the keyboard when you feel you need to, look away when you are confident that you will not make too many mistakes. Occasionally check you have the correct fingers on the keys and that your pivot fingers have not strayed on to the wrong keys. This will ensure the avoidance of most errors right from the start.

Some touch-typing methods advocate 'not looking at the keyboard' right from the very first lesson, and believe this will encourage a good habit. I believe no one wants bad habits and that glancing/looking at the keyboard will decrease with experience and keyboard proficiency. Not looking and attempting to memorize the entire keyboard so soon in order to recall, perfectly, the location of each key is not an easy task. If peeking helps, then do it.

● EXAMPLE

Left hand words	Right hand words
fred fred fred	jimmy jimmy jimmy
deaf deaf deaf	lolly lolly lolly
seed seed seed	poppy poppy poppy
great great great	hum hum hum
sweet sweet sweet	nim nim nim
beggar beggar beggar	jumpy jumpy jumpy

● THE ALPHABET

abcdefghijklmnopqrstuvwxyz

a b c d e f g h i j k l m

n o p q r s t u v w x y z

● EXPLANATION

Warm up just to get the feel of the typewriter/keyboard all over again. The left hand and right hand words are quite easy to type, but do require a bit of stretching and thinking.

When you know that a whole series of words will only require one hand, it is easier to concentrate your thoughts on just one area of the keyboard and help speed up the process of learning where the keys are.

Don't forget to replace all your fingers on their home keys at the end of every word.

The alphabet should be a bit of fun. Don't hurry, make sure you are using the correct fingers and, if necessary, look at the chart and diagram – whichever you find easier to learn from.

The second alphabet with the space between each letter will keep your right thumb busy, but will also help to make the insertion of a space within your typing an automatic process.

If you feel keen, you may do the lesson a second time, but don't bother to correct any mistakes. Just notice what they were and try to work out why you made them – that's half way to making sure you don't do it again.

WORDS WITH A CAPITAL LETTER

Now that you have become acquainted with the keys on your keyboard, and your space bar, it's time to think about typing your first few words with a capital letter. The following exercises are aimed at increasing the proficiency of each hand. In time it will be just as easy to type words that use both hands, within the space of one word.

○ First, as always from this session onwards, warm up with the alphabet, without spaces and then again with a space between each letter. Type it slowly and carefully with the correct fingers. Look for the keys if you need to; in time you will do this less and less often.

○ Type the following left hand words three times each, without a capital letter for the time being.

actress   access   abstract   abate

bat   beaver   better   brew

carefree   cassette   craft   created

○ Type the following right hand words three times each, similarly without a capital letter.

hill   holy   hump   hymn

ill   imply   ink   inn

join   jolly   july   jump

And now, the moment you have been waiting for, the 'Great Performing Capital Letter'. In order to make a capital letter you need to depress the shift key which is always operated by the little fingers. Left hand words require the use of the right hand shift key, operated by Riv. Likewise, right hand words require the use of the left hand shift key, operated by Liv. Simple! Do not lock the shift key in position, this will make the entire word come out in capitals and this is not what is intended for this session.

o   Feel your shift keys. First the left one, then the right one. When you are doing this be sure to use your Li and Ri fingers as temporary pivot points on their respective home keys. Once you have depressed the shift key, typed your capital letter, you can then bring your little finger back to its own pivot point/home key.

o   Type the following left hand words three times each, but start each with a capital letter.

Actress   Access   Abstract   Abate

Bat   Beaver   Better   Brew

Carefree   Cassette   Craft   Created

o   Type these right hand words, again three times each and start each with a capital letter (a capital letter is also known as an upper-case letter).

Hill   Holy   Hump   Hymn

Ill   Imply   Ink   Inn

Join   Jolly   July   Jump

● EXAMPLE

abcdefghijklmnopqrstuvwxyz
a b c d e f g h i j k l m
n o p q r s t u v w x y z

Left hand words

actress actress actress
access access access
abstract abstract abstract
abate abate abate
bat bat bat
beaver beaver beaver
better better better
brew brew brew
carefree carefree carefree
cassette cassette cassette
craft craft craft
created created created

Left hand words with a
capital letter

Actress Actress Actress
Access Access Access
Abstract Abstract Abstract
Abate Abate Abate
Bat Bat Bat
Beaver Beaver Beaver
Better Better Better
Brew Brew Brew
Carefree Carefree Carefree
Cassette Cassette Cassette
Craft Craft Craft
Created Created Created

Right hand words

hill hill hill
holy holy holy
hump hump hump
hymn hymn hymn
ill ill ill
imply imply imply
ink ink ink
inn inn inn
join join join
jolly jolly jolly
july july july
jump jump jump

Right hand words with a capital letter

Hill Hill Hill
Holy Holy Holy
Hump Hump Hump
Hymn Hymn Hymn
Ill Ill Ill
Imply Imply Imply
Ink Ink Ink
Inn Inn Inn
Join Join Join
Jolly Jolly Jolly
July July July
Jump Jump Jump

• EXPLANATION

Personally, I don't believe anyone can learn to type quickly or to control their keyboard if they practise typing lines of gobbledygook. It makes no sense to the eye or brain and makes the anticipation of the next letter nearly impossible, and then attempting to spot your mistakes is like trying to spot a Polish spelling mistake (if you are not Polish, that is!).

So we start off with proper words. If you know how to spell a short word and know that it will only need the use of a single hand, then proficiency at that word and, more important, the use of that hand will increase at a greater pace than typing the traditional 'asdf ;lkj' rows. Those of you that are ambidextrous, or play the piano, will find both the left and right hand exercises as easy as each other. Those of you that are definitely right handed may take a little time to get used to using the left hand, especially the little finger. Likewise, those of you that are left handed may find it takes a while to get used to using the little finger of the right hand. However, within a few days this awkwardness will pass.

YOUR FIRST SENTENCE

○ As always, look through the session and example and explanation before doing any typing.

○ Type the alphabet to get into the swing of knowing where the letters are again.

○ Do this once more but this time insert a space between each letter.

○ Finally, type the alphabet with a comma after each letter and a space after each comma.

For some reason, some letters that were very easy to locate over the last few days may suddenly become 'lost' again. Don't worry, they will stick in your memory eventually.

○ Now type the following left hand phrases three times each.

beware a bearded bat

a tax retreat

a vast secret target

○ Type the following right hand phrases three times each.

joy in july

my lump on my lip

no hook on my loop

○ Type the following left hand words three times each.

Data   Dearest   Detect

Eastwards   Erase   Estate

Fact   Feared   Feeder

○   Now type the following right hand words three times each.

Killjoy   Kink   Knoll
Link   Lion   Loop
Million   Moon   Monopoly

●   EXAMPLE

```
abcdefghijklmnopqrstuvwxyz
a b c d e f g h i j k l m
n o p q r s t u v w x y z
a, b, c, d, e, f, g, h, i, j, k, l, m,
n, o, p, q, r, s, t, u, v, w, x, y, z,


beware a bearded bat
beware a bearded bat
beware a bearded bat
a tax retreat
a tax retreat
a tax retreat
a vast secret target
a vast secret target
a vast secret target


joy in july
joy in july
joy in july
my lump on my lip
my lump on my lip
my lump on my lip
no hook on my loop
no hook on my loop
no hook on my loop


Data Data Data
Dearest Dearest Dearest
Detect Detect Detect
```

```
Eastwards Eastwards Eastwards
Erase Erase Erase
Estate Estate Estate
Fact Fact Fact
Feared Feared Feared
Feeder Feeder Feeder

Killjoy Killjoy Killjoy
Kink Kink Kink
Knoll Knoll Knoll
Link Link Link
Lion Lion Lion
Loop Loop Loop
Million Million Million
Moon Moon Moon
Monopoly Monopoly Monopoly
```

• EXPLANATION

You may find that each session is now getting slightly longer than the one before. This is to build up your keyboard stamina.

The shift key, the space bar and comma need to become automatic. Suddenly it will all fall into place! Typing the alphabet in this way helps to learn to do commas and spaces automatically. The left and right hand words are helping you to improve your dexterity in each hand without having to think about swopping to the other hand in mid-word. This skill will be practised later on in another session. Likewise, the left and right hand sentences help you to establish rhythm (slow as it may be at the beginning) and flow in typing a sentence. It also helps to keep the thumb in good working order!

Although you are at present only typing words that require the use of a single hand, both hands must be poised on the keyboard – in readiness for the day when you will type with both hands for a single word.

• A FRIENDLY WORD OF ADVICE

Some groups of letters will now become more familiar to you, 'eg', 'er', 'est', 'ed', 'ion', 'oo', 'in' etc. However, you may still experience the odd hiccup with the upper-case letters and some of the rarely used keys. At times things may get out of synch, letters get typed the wrong way round, capitals are misplaced, or some letters (on manual typewriters) will be typed in mid-air, way above the normal typing line. Don't fret, don't worry, in a very short time you will depress the correct shift key and type the letter in upper case followed very fluently by the next lower case letter, with nothing going awry. Hard to believe, but it comes to us all in the end.

A common mistake is to hold the shift key down for too long, ending up with several upper-case letters in a single word that only required the first letter to be a capital, or to let the shift key lock, thus ending up with several words in a sentence typed in upper case. So check regularly that you are still on the correct pivot point and home keys and that the shift key hasn't been accidentally locked, and that you haven't come off the edge of your sheet of paper!

LET'S USE BOTH HANDS

o As before, warm up with a run through of the alphabet, in lower case, separating each letter with a comma and a space.

o Now, using the shift key, type the alphabet in upper case, separating each letter with only a space. Be careful not to lock the shift key (this would make it too easy for you) and remember that for a left hand letter you engage the shift key with the little finger of the right hand and vice versa, and at the same time, use your Li (or Ri) finger as a temporary pivot point by keeping it firmly placed on its own home key. Be careful not to accidentally type this key in your keenness to keep hold of it!!

When you get to type 'P', for example,

Liv will be on the left shift key
Li will be poised on the 'F' key

Ri will be poised on the 'J' key
Rii and Riii will be off their keys, 'K' and 'L'
Riv will be on and typing the 'P' key.

It all seems rather complicated when broken down into segments, but there is a systematic logic to it which is what makes it all fall into place in the end!!

o As an easier exercise, type the numbers 1 to 0.

o And now for some words: Type the following left hand words three times each. (Note there are no capital letters to type just yet.)

**garage   garbage   geared   radar   rate   reacted   regret
safest   scattered   seaweed**

○ Type the following right hand words three times each.

mop my nippy noon noun nylon onlook opinion pillion pony

Don't despair if you feel you are typing ever so slowly – most of these words are deliberately tricky and would cause the most experienced keyboard controller to slow down and think twice.

○ Have a go at typing the following left hand mini sentences, as always three times each in single line spacing, with an upper-case letter at the start of each sentence.

Cabbage cafe.   We regret we feasted.
Barefaced bat breeder.

○ Do the same for the right hand, three mini sentences, three times each.

Pull my puny pony uphill.   Moon nymph on my lily.

No nippy noon in July.

○ Now for something slightly different; two-handed phrases, one left hand word, one right hand word. As usual type them three times each.

You beware.   Nylon sweater.   Cave nymph.

○ Type the following left hand sentence three times, not forgetting the upper-case letters.

We barefaced bat breeders regret we feasted at Cabbage Cafe.

○ Here is a right hand sentence to be typed three times.

Moon nymph pull my puny pony uphill in nippy July.

○ At last, the long-awaited two-handed performance! Each word is still only typed with a single hand, but there are both left and right hand words in these sentences. Need I say, type them three times each?

Eat watercress in July.

My nylon sweater was tattered in a cave.

Taste my pink seaweed tart Polly.

• EXAMPLE

a, b, c, d, e, f, g, h, i, j, k, l, m,
n, o, p, q, r, s, t, u, v, w, x, y, z,

A, B, C, D, E, F, G, H, I, J, K, L, M,
N, O, P, Q, R, S, T, U, V, W, X, Y, Z,

1234567890

garage garage garage
garbage garbage garbage
geared geared geared
radar radar radar
rate rate rate
reacted reacted reacted
regret regret regret
safest safest safest
scattered scattered scattered
seaweed seaweed seaweed

mop mop mop
my my my
nippy nippy nippy
noon noon noon
noun noun noun
nylon nylon nylon
onlook onlook onlook
opinion opinion opinion
pillion pillion pillion
pony pony pony

Cabbage cafe.
Cabbage cafe.
Cabbage cafe.
We regret we feasted.
We regret we feasted.
We regret we feasted.

Barefaced bat breeder.
Barefaced bat breeder.
Barefaced bat breeder.

Pull my puny pony uphill.
Pull my puny pony uphill.
Pull my puny pony uphill.
Moon nymph on my lily.
Moon nymph on my lily.
Moon nymph on my lily.
No nippy noon in July.
No nippy noon in July.
No nippy noon in July.

You beware.
You beware.
You beware.
Nylon sweater.
Nylon sweater.
Nylon sweater.
Cave nymph.
Cave nymph.
Cave nymph.

We barefaced bat breeders regret we
feasted at Cabbage Cafe.
We barefaced bat breeders regret we
feasted at Cabbage Cafe.
We barefaced bat breeders regret we
feasted at Cabbage Cafe.

Moon nymph pull my puny pony uphill
in nippy July.
Moon nymph pull my puny pony uphill
in nippy July.
Moon nymph pull my puny pony uphill
in nippy July.

```
Eat watercress in July.
Eat watercress in July.
Eat watercress in July.
My nylon sweater was tattered in a cave.
My nylon sweater was tattered in a cave.
My nylon sweater was tattered in a cave.
Taste my pink seaweed tart Polly.
Taste my pink seaweed tart Polly.
Taste my pink seaweed tart Polly.
```

● EXPLANATION

The sessions from now on will aim to warm you up, to get you into the swing of typing each of the letters in upper and lower case and then to exercise the left and right hand separately.

It will begin to feel easier to use one hand to type one word and the other hand to type the next, if you are already familiar with some of the words from previous exercises. Knowing a short sentence off by heart, prior to typing it, will help you to anticipate which fingers you will need to use and help you to concentrate on typing the words with the correct fingers. For fun, I have introduced some long left and right hand sentences, these should help you to become more confident about typing passages from books or newspapers at a later date.

You will soon realize that the length of a word or the length of a sentence has little bearing on how difficult it is to type. Some of the shorter sentences with shorter words are some of the trickiest – they are deliberately so. When the time comes to type ordinary text, it won't seem half as difficult as you were anticipating, if you have typed these 'short and sticky' sentences.

REFERENCE SECTION
(Not essential reading for the sessions)

● **SPOTS AND SPACES**

(This is not a session, just information for you to read at your leisure and at your own pace. If you wish to skip reading this section and move straight on to Session 7 you may do so; it will not mar your performance in the ensuing sessions.)

Punctuation is a matter of style and preference which will be dealt with later, but to begin with let's sort out the spots, dots and spaces that crop up in typing.

○ The first thing to remember is that full stops and question marks need two spaces after them, before starting the next sentence. In fact, anything that ends a sentence needs two spaces after it! Including exclamation marks!! Colons are also followed by two spaces.

○ The second point to remember is that after typing a semi-colon, a comma or a dash within a sentence, you leave just one space after it, before typing the next word.

○ The third point to remember is that everything else is typed immediately before or after a character, that is without a space; this includes apostrophe marks, quotation marks, brackets, hyphens, pound and dollar signs, percentage marks, the lot!

So it's as simple as that. Remember the first two rules and the third will follow logically.

When a (word) is typed within a bracket or a single or double "quotation mark", there is no space immediately after the opening bracket or

quotation mark nor before the closing bracket or
quotation mark. New sentences start 2 spaces.
after the full stop, exclamation/question mark
of the last one! The solidus sign has no space
either side of it and a dash - requires one
space before and after it, unlike the comma
which needs no space before it, but a single one
after it. The '£' or '$' sign is always typed
immediately infront of the figure it represents,
essentially to prevent fraud.

● PUNCTUATION OF ADDRESSES

The punctuation of names and addresses comes in two main
styles; 'open' and 'full'. An example of open punctuation
would be the following:

```
Mr R W Brown               R W Brown Esq
8 Highridge Street         8 Highridge St
                   or
Lamptown                   Lamptown
Essex      AB1 2JK         Essex      AB1 2JK
```

An example of full punctuation would be as follows:

```
Mr. R. W. Brown,           R. W. Brown, Esq.,
8, Highridge Street,       8, Highridge St.,
                   or
Lamptown,                  Lamptown,
Essex.     AB1 2JK         Essex.      AB1 2JK
```

Preference is personal but open is modern!

Notice that there is only *one* space after the full stops in Mr
Brown's name and this is the only exception to the full stop
rule as outlined earlier. Frequently, people tend to leave the
spaces out altogether when typing in full punctuation style;
however, it's wrong and it looks odd. Mr.R.W.Brown (or any
variation on this theme) is incorrect because the space has
been left out between the full stops after 'Mr' and the letter 'R'
and the letter 'W'.

● LINE SPACING

This is a simple term referring to the amount of space between the lines in a section of typing. Normally, letters are typed in single line spacing.

Single line spacing is in effect two half lines: $(\frac{1}{2} + \frac{1}{2} = 1)$!! Although the typewriter is capable of typing in half line spacing it is never used – if it were, it would give the effect of one line of type giving a piggy-back to the one above it – however, it enables the typewriter to type in 1½ and 2½ lines spacing and to insert an extra ½ line spacing when necessary.

The following line of type has been
deliberately typed in half line spacing
in order to illustrate why it is never
used by keyboard controllers.

So, if nothing is ever typed in half line spacing, and most things are typed in single line spacing, what is typed in more than single line spacing?

Manuscripts, scripts, drafts of documents etc are often typed in double line spacing. It makes it easier to insert omissions and to correct mistakes. Similarly, triple line spacing is used, though less frequently, for the same sort of work, but it must be borne in mind that it does use up the paper at an incredible rate and if your corrections are not prolific, it may be considered excessive.

This line of type is

separated from the

next line by double

line spacing. It

makes it *much* /easier for

the keyboard con-

troller to insert

This line of type is

as you will notice

separated /from the

next typed line by

triple line spacing

and it makes it much

48

extra words between   easier for the insert-

the lines.
                             ion of lengthy hand-

                             written omissions.

Modern letter style requires paragraphs to be separated by
double line spacing (with or without indentation which is
optional and will be dealt with later on).

A tip to remember is that any paragraph separation is double
whatever the amount of line spacing you have been using for
the body of the typed text. So if work has been typed in 1½ line
spacing, leave three lines before starting the next paragraph.
Similarly, if the main body of the typewritten work has been
done in double line spacing, it follows that you leave four lines
between each paragraph. Triple line spacing requires six lines
between the end of one paragraph and the start of the next.
Simple mathematics!

● UNDERLINING

Sometimes this process is known as underscoring, but whatever you call it, it is still achieved by using the __ character. On
some keyboards it will be found as the upper-case character
on the '6' key, on others it may be the upper-case character of
the dash key, but do not confuse it with the dash sign which
is smaller and is typed higher up on your typing line.

● HOW TO UNDERLINE

Type your heading, then return your typing point to the start
of the heading, engage the shift key and lock it, underline using
the correct key for this function.

You do not need to turn up a line or half a line to do this – if
you do have to, it is because you are using the wrong key –

this is a common mistake; people attempt to use the dash character to underline a word or heading but it will invariably involve turning up to the next line, or jiggling with the paper or some other time-consuming fiddly process. All in all it is a bit of a wobbly mess – take my advice don't even try it this way. A useful tip to remember at this point is that when commencing a paragraph after an underlined heading, add an extra half line space between the heading and the following paragraph. This will help to maintain a uniform distance between each paragraph.

If your paragraphs are to be separated by double line spacing, then leave 2½ lines after the underlined heading. The reason for this is that the process of underlining inadvertently drops the depth of the typed line by precisely half a line. Therefore, when you start the new paragraph you will need to compensate for this in order for this particular paragraph and all subsequent paragraphs to look equally spaced out! Although you do not turn up half a line to type the underlining, it still appears to drop the bottom edge of the typed line. This is a deliberate typing quirk. It merely prevents the heading or whatever has been underlined from giving the appearance of having been crossed out! Confused? Look at the following illustrations.

UNDERLINE
This next line of
type is 1 line below
the heading.

UNDERLINE

This next line of
type is 1½ lines
below the heading.

UNDERLINE

The next line of
type is 2 lines
below the heading.

UNDERLINE

This next line of
type is 2½ lines
below the heading.

UNDERLINE

This next line of
type is 3 lines
below the heading.

You can judge for yourself which line spacing looks most appropriate for your own particular needs.

● NUMBERS AND SUMS

One of the most difficult things for all keyboard operators to deal with is the laying out of columns of figures with sub-total and full total lines in the right place. The point to remember is that all underlining lowers the typed line by a half line. Without turning the typing line up at all the underline appears at the following level for this line ___. See how it seems to be half a line below everything else. In addition the next line of typing appears to bump its head on the underlined section. This, then, is the crux of the underlining problem. Bear this in mind always when underlining words or figures and your problems are gone.

So let's see how this amazing piece of advice works in practice:

(A)	NAMES	(B)	NAMES	(C)	NAMES
	Andrew		Andrew		Andrew
	Sarah		Sarah		Sarah
	Paul		Paul		Paul
	Jane		Jane		Jane

In examples (A), (B) and (C) all the names are in single line spacing, but each commences after the underlined heading in differing line spacing: (A) is single line spacing, (B) is 1½ lines spacing and (C) is 2 lines spacing.

If the names were typed in double line spacing it would be necessary to separate the underlined heading from the first name by 2½ lines spacing, e.g.:

(D) <u>NAMES</u>

    Andrew

    Sarah

    Paul

    Jane

This allows the heading and each subsequent name to be equi-distant from one another.

The same principle applies in typing columns of figures:

(A)	123	(B)	123
	100		100
	123		123
	100		100
	___		___
	446		446
	___		___

(A) has been typed in single line spacing throughout and, as you can see, the total figure and underlining look misaligned. In (B) the figures have been typed in single line spacing, then the typing line has been turned up only ½ a line to type the first underline, then 1½ lines to type the total, then ½ line to type the final underline. As you can see the overall depth of the column is the same, but the layout is much more pleasing to the eye. You would employ the same underlining measurements if your columns were typed in 1½ lines spacing.

If, however, your columns of figures were typed in double line spacing, then the first underline is typed after turning up only a single line, then turn up two lines for the total figure, then a single line to type the final underline, as follows:

(C)   123

       100

       123

       100
       ___

       446
       ___

But what about double underlining, ===== like so!
Type the 'equals' character several times, ===, then go back
to the beginning of the line, move the typing point forward
just half a space and repeat the character several times in order
to fill in the spaces between each 'equals' sign – hey presto, a
double underline. But, when it comes to typing this particular
line it is essential to turn up an additional half line before typing; this is because this particular character does not drop half
a line like the underscore line does (in fact the underscore
is the only character on the keyboard to drop in this way).
Therefore, you need to turn up a whole line after typing the
total figure if your column is in single or 1½ lines spacing,
or alternatively, if the column has been typed in double line
spacing, you need to turn up 1½ lines before typing the final
double underlining, as follows:

(D)   123

       100

       123

       100
       ___

       446
       ===

• THE HALF-SPACE KEY

Well, that's all very well, but my typewriter doesn't have a half space key! It's an old manual, highly trustworthy, it's got all its letters but no half-space key. In that case, your half-space key is immediately under your right thumb – it is the space bar.

Press it down and do not release it. See where it brings your typing point to. Now release it – look how it has moved on – half a space with each movement. Electronic typewriters cannot do this, nor most electric typewriters, hence the introduction of the half-space key. So if you want to move the typing point on just half a space, press down on the space bar and hold it in this position until you have typed the letter(s) or word that you want to squeeze into a small space. It may mean holding the space bar with both thumbs so that you can type with both hands, without releasing the space bar. If necessary, a whole word can be typed with just half a space between each letter.

Letterbox   this takes up the space of five characters only.

Letter box in the normal way these words take up ten
            character spaces.

The process is slow, but it can be useful as a short cut to correcting something that doesn't require perfect presentation.

After typing each letter, back space one whole space, then forward half a space, with either your space bar or half-space key, then type the next letter and repeat this process until each letter has been typed.

54

• CENTRED HEADINGS   (And How to Make Them)

CENTRED HEADINGS

(And How to Make Them)

How smart – to have your name, address or title of a piece of work neatly centred over the width of your page. It's easier than it looks! And this is how it is done.

o   First know the size of your paper, most importantly the width. A4 is the most common size of typing paper and is 100 characters wide (if your typing pitch is 12 characters to the inch – pitch will be explained later in more detail).

o   Find the middle point on the paper and bring your typing point to this position. If you have inserted your paper at the 0 point, at the left hand edge, this will be at the 50 position, otherwise you may measure this position by hand with a ruler.

o   From this point, back space one place for every two letters/spaces in your title. Do not include the odd letter if at the end of the name or title there should be one letter left over. So, for the words 'centred headings' as above, you would need to back space 8 places from the centre of the page.

o   Say to yourself 'CE', back space, 'NT', back space, 'RE', back space, 'D' and space, back space. 'HE' back space, 'AD' back space, 'IN' back space, 'GS' back space, as you go along the line. As long as you back space once every time you tell yourself to do so you will end up in the right place. And wherever you do end up, somewhere left of where you began (eight places to be precise in this instance), commence typing the heading and it should finish up as perfectly centred.

A N D   H O W   T O   M A K E   T H E M

The title above is more interesting to look at and attracts your attention. It too is very easy to centre. From the centre point on the paper, back space once for every letter and space occurring in the title. For this heading 'And How to Make Them' you will need to back space twenty spaces from the middle of the page. Then type each letter followed by a space. The space between each word must have an additional space after it, so in all you will leave three spaces after the end of each word before starting the next word.

In summary, there is no counting of letters and dividing by two and subtracting from 50 and adding to 0 and multiplying by your aged aunt's date of birth! The method outlined here is much simpler than that. Just back space from the centre of the page, once for every couple of characters/spaces by spelling out the heading to yourself as you go backwards along the line, or alternatively, for the expanded heading, once for every single character and space.

● MARGINS AND TABULATIONS

These sound like a high-street department store or a comedy double act. What are they doing in this book then?

A margin separates the two extreme edges of your typed text from the edge of your paper or computer-display area. Normally, the left hand margin is at least two or three centimetres wide and the right hand margin is just a little narrower, e.g. three or five characters less than the left margin, nothing more. This helps to balance the finished appearance of the page because it is most unlikely that you will end up with every word finishing on the same spot at the right hand edge. You attempt to get as close to it as possible; sometimes to do this you may need to hyphenate a word. Take a suitable breaking point, either at the end of a syllable or after double letters (for example, poss-ible, instruc-tion, letter-ing, insert-ed etc. The hyphen (the dash character) is typed immediately after the first part of the word, at the right hand edge, never at the left hand margin.

Different typewriters have different means of setting the margins, so it would be pointless to try to explain setting them for any particular typewriter, word-processor or computer. It would probably not be the way to do it for your machine.

Let us assume you have found out how to set the margins; you now need to know what tabulation ('tab' for short) means. If you were typing several columns of figures, names etc, the starting point of each separate column would be called the tab point. By depressing the tab key at the points required and thus setting the tabs, you can speed up the process of arriving at the starting point of each column. Using this method you work through the columns row by row, moving from left to right across the page, rather than typing first one column, then the next.

This method has two benefits: first, it removes the need to type each column separately which can make it difficult to align the columns, and second, it removes the need to press the space bar frantically in order to get to the next column's starting point. After typing the first name/figure in the first column, press the 'tab forward' key which automatically moves the typing point to the start of the next column, type the first name of the second column and repeat the process until you have worked across the entire width of the page and typed in the first name of every column, having arrived at the start of each by pressing the tab forward key.

```
John        Mary        Peter
Jane        Sue         Bob
Katey       Lily        Betty
Tina        Sara        Gary
```

Tab points were set at the 'J' point in John for column one, at the 'M' point in Mary for column two and at the 'P' point in Peter for column 3. The names were typed in the following order;

John, Mary, Peter, Jane, Sue, Bob, Katey, Lily, Betty, Tina, Sara, Gary.

Some people's tabs look much neater and better than others. What is their secret? They simply follow the rule of always leaving an odd number of spaces between each column, e.g. three, five, seven, nine or more spaces, and they keep the chosen number of spaces between each column consistent throughout the body of a work. If the words in your columns are of varying length, use the longest word in each column as the right hand edge of that column and work from that point to count to the next tab point.

```
January       April       July          October
February      May         August        November
March         June        September     December
```

In the above example there are five character spaces after the last letter of the longest word and before the first letter in the next column. In detail this means that there are five spaces after the 'Y' in February to separate it from the next column and five spaces after the 'L' in April before the start of the next column and, likewise, five spaces after the 'R' in September before the final column. In other words, you leave five spaces after the longest word in each column in order to determine the tab point for the next column. As you can probably guess, this must be calculated prior to typing out your list either as a handwritten or typed draft.

● **CONTENTS AND INDEX PAGES**

If you have sufficient space, always attempt to type a contents/index page in double or triple-line spacing. To help your eyes move from the title of a page to its number, type a few dots at regular intervals along the line. Your tabulation skill will come in very handy here.

With your tabulation key clear all old tabs and then set new ones, at the start of each set of dots; you may use your personal preference here, but I think the most attractive distance between each tab point is eight spaces, or three dots followed by five spaces, but feel free to experiment with style to suit your own preferences.

Remember these rules:
○ Don't switch from a two-dot style back to a three-dot style and so on. Be consistent.
○ Make sure the columns of dots are exactly under one another.
○ If the first series of dots commences less than three spaces after the last letter of the title, then leave out this first set of dots.

```
French Onion Soup      ...        ...      Page 14

Leek and Onion Soup               ...      Page 16

Potato Soup            ...        ...      Page 18
```

Notice that the set of dots immediately under the first set in the 'French Onion Soup' line has been omitted from the 'Leek and Onion Soup' line because it would be too close to the words 'Onion Soup'; it is less obtrusive to leave it out!

● SQUEEZING IN THE MISSED-OUT LETTER

Now that you are becoming a little more confident on your keyboard, chances are that you will occasionally leave out a letter from a word. How do we solve this minor problem? If on your machine it is no trouble to retype a section, or on your word-processor a simple instruction eradicates the mistake, all is well and good, but if you have made the mistake on a common-or-garden typewriter, manual or electric, and didn't spot it at the time, this is not quite as simple to solve, though it can be done.

```
The bok I read was lousy.
The book I read was lousy.
```

In the above example you can see that the correct version takes up no extra character in the length of the line; you will also notice that all the words except the word 'book' are precisely in alignment with the words in the line above. These are the steps to making the correction:

(1) white out the word 'bok' and allow the fluid to dry!

(2) bring your typing point to the letter 'e' in the word 'The';

(3) press the space bar once to simulate typing the letter 'e' then, press your half-space key. This will leave just half a space between the words 'The' and 'book'; and

(4) now type the word 'book'.

You will now find that there is just half a space between the end of the word 'book' and the word 'I'. The error hardly shows.

Don't forget that if you have no half-space key on your keyboard you can use your space bar instead, as was explained earlier. If you do, you will need to hold it in the depressed position with both thumbs for every single letter in the word. Release and depress before each letter until you have finished typing the word. If you do accidentally release it you will inadvertently introduce an additional half space within the letters of the word 'book' and that in itself will look like an error! If you are in a hurry or the word is rather long or you don't want to use white-out or the presentation of your work does not need to be perfect, then it is possible to squeeze in the extra letter like this:

waiter

The mistake obviously shows (and more so in some words than in others), but at least it is a correction, without which the sense of a sentence may be changed quite considerably, e.g. water/waiter!!

This correction is done as follows:

(1) bring the typing point in line with the letter prior to the omitted letter;

(2) press the half-space key; and

(3) type the letter that has been left out.

Similarly, if you have left out the space between two words, it is possible to use the same principle to remedy this particular fault.

```
The fat catwas left out in the rain.

The fat cat was left out in the rain.
```

   (1) White out the word 'was' and allow to dry;
   (2) bring your typing point to the letter 't' in 'cat';
   (3) press the space bar once to simulate typing the letter 't';
   (4) press the half-space key; and
   (5) type the word 'was'.

You will again find that there is just a half space either side of the word 'was' and the error has been disguised. If you do not wish to use white-out or don't have the time to use this method or presentation is not that important, you can merely insert a solidus sign between the 't' in 'cat' and the 'w' in 'was', as follows:

```
The fat cat/was left out in the rain.
```

One point worth remembering is that some mistakes will look better corrected one way rather than another. Further, some individual words look better corrected in one way than in another – this just depends on the combination of the letters – it's the luck of the draw. Anyway, in time, it won't happen so often!!

• SPOT THE DELIBERATE MISTAKE

17 Longbridge Street
Westcliffe
Dorset
BH23 4ZZ

8 June 1987

Mr.A.Brown
'Crock Place",
16 Townham Road.
  Salisbury
 Wilts.

Dear Mr. Brown,
              Thank you for your letter of 6
Juen. I would be delighted to attend for an
interview at 1100 A.m.
    I hope you won't askme to do a typing test
or anything like that because I'M no good when
I'mm nervous !

        Last week I had an interview with a
company on the other side of town,probably one
of your rivals,but, a nyway i didnt get the job
in the end. Not that I minded very much because
I would rather work for your company anyhow.
Yours faithfully,

    Miss Stake (Sally)

PS.I've enclosed a photograph of myself, holding my d budgies first egg which never hatched
out after all. Please send it back xwhen you
have looked at it.

● ERRORS MADE BY MISS STAKE

Poor Sally, she made many errors in her letter to Mr Brown. Why?

Her style was inconsistent and she made the obvious amateur blunders.

Her corrections showed.

She forgot to leave a space after her commas.

She forgot to leave one space after the full stop punctuation in Mr Brown's name.

She used double quotation marks round the name of his house instead of single ones.

Her paragraphs were not separated by double-line spacing.

Sally's indented lines at the start of each of her paragraphs were not aligned with one another. They should have been five spaces in from the left-hand margin.

The time of her interview was a bit of a botch job. Sally left out the full stop between 11 and 00 and the a.m. should have been in lower case.

Sally's exclamation mark should be immediately after the 's' in 'nervous'.

At the end of her sentences she sometimes forgot to leave two spaces after a full stop.

The word 'Faithfully' should only be used in letters that start with 'Dear Sir or Madam'.

Her name was typed in the wrong order, and her letter contained spelling mistakes.

She left out the word 'Enclosure' or its abbreviated form 'Enc' from the bottom of her letter.

Surprisingly, these are only a few of Sally's mistakes. Good for you if you have spotted more of them. Although Miss Sally Stake's letter was a rather bad one, it does look better if it is typed properly. The two examples, in differing styles, illustrate this point.

- **CORRECTED VERSION OF MISS STAKE'S LETTER (I)**

- **OPEN PUNCTUATION WITH BLOCKED PARAGRAPHS**

                17 LONGBRIDGE STREET, WESTCLIFFE
                        DORSET BH23 4ZZ

8 June 1987

Mr A Brown
'Crock Place'
16 Townham Road
Salisbury
Wilts

Dear Mr Brown

Thank you for your letter of 6 June. I would be
delighted to attend for an interview at 11.00 am.
I hope you won't ask me to do a typing test or
anything like that because I'm no good when I'm
nervous!

Last week I had an interview with a company on
the other side of town, probably one of your
rivals, but, anyway I didn't get the job in the
end. Not that I minded very much because I would
rather work for your company anyhow.

Yours sincerely

Sally Stake (Miss)

PS I've enclosed a photograph of myself, holding
my budgie's first egg which never hatched out
after all. Please send it back when you have
looked at it.

Enc

17, Longbridge Street,
Westcliffe,
Dorset.
BH23 4ZZ.

8th June, 1987.

Mr. A. Brown,
'Crock Place',
16, Townham Road,
Salisbury,
Wilts.

Dear Mr. Brown,

Thank you for your letter of 6th June. I would be delighted to attend for an interview at 11.00 a.m. I hope you won't ask me to do a typing test or anything like that because I'm no good when I'm nervous!

Last week I had an interview with a company on the other side of town, probably one of your rivals, but, anyway I didn't get the job in the end. Not that I minded very much because I would rather work for your company anyhow.

Yours sincerely,

Sally Stake (Miss)

PS. I've enclosed a photograph of myself, holding my budgie's first egg which never hatched out after all. Please send it back when you have looked at it.

Enc.

• ENVELOPES ADDRESSED BY MISS STAKE

```
Mrs., C.Leggs,
'  Fisherman's Cottagg"

Little Drayton,
 LYme on the Mould
Dorset  BH22LL
```

```
        Mrs.C.Leggs,
        "Fisherman's Cottage",
            Little Drayton
              Dymeon the Mould
                  Dorset
                      BH2 "LL
```

Again, as you can see, Sally has used every style and mistake under the sun. The corrected versions of her envelopes follow.

• CORRECTED VERSION OF MISS STAKE'S ENVELOPES

• OPEN PUNCTUATION AND FULLY BLOCKED LINES

```
Mrs C Leggs
'Fisherman's Cottage'
Little Drayton
LYME ON THE MOULD
Dorset       BH2 2LL
```

No full stops or commas.
No indentation of lines.
Single line spacing.
Postal town in upper case to help sorting at the post office.
Post code on the same line as the county but separated by at least five character spaces.

• FULL PUNCTUATION AND INDENTED LINES

```
Mrs. C. Leggs,
 'Fisherman's Cottage',
    Little Drayton,
      LYME ON THE MOULD,
        Dorset.
          BH2 2LL.
```

Full stops after each abbreviated term.
Commas after each line.
Post town in upper case.
Full stop after the county.
Consistent indentation of three spaces for the start of each line, after the starting point of the previous line.

The above are not fixed blueprints and there are other variations:

    fully blocked addresses can be typed in open or full punctuation;

    the post code can be typed on a separate line in any style;

    indented addresses may be typed in open punctuation.

The address must be typed half-way down the envelope with a margin of at least four centimetres.

On very large envelopes type the address in double-line spacing, as near to the centre of the envelope as possible.

• A QUICK AND TIDY LETTER STYLE

The simplest, quickest and tidiest letter to type is fully blocked with open punctuation. The less spots, dots, indentations and hyphenations etc., the quicker the letter is to type and the tidier the appearance of the finished article. If you haven't got headed note paper, centre your address across the top of the first page, about three centimetres down from the top of the page.

```
            17 Longbridge Street, Westcliffe,
                    Dorset BH23 4ZZ

                          or

            17 LONGBRIDGE STREET, WESTCLIFFE,
                    DORSET BH23 4ZZ
                    Tel 01-733 9999


Mrs L Pondoling
4 Beech Tree Lane
WINTERTON
Surrey     BU1 1OA

9 September 1987

Dear Linda

Thank you for your recent letter.  I'm sorry I
haven't written to you in ages.

Yes, we'd love to come and stay in your new
home for a few days at the end of the month.

The kittens have grown into huge monsters with
appetites to match - we'll bring you one if you
insist.

Love and kisses,
```

• A NEAT RIGHT EDGE

How do some people manage to type their address on the right hand side of their paper and get each of the lines to end up finishing at the same point? Sally Stake obviously tried, but only ended up with a wobbly and uneven right hand margin, as below:

```
            17 Longbridge Street
                      Westcliffe
            Dorset
                 BH23 4ZZ
```

What Sally was aiming for was this:

```
            17 Longbridge Street
                      Westcliffe
                          Dorset
                       BH23 4ZZ


                     8 June 1987
```

It looks smart and efficient, and it is easy when you know how!!

The following is a list of the steps to doing it: **(1)** bring your typing point to the exact spot you would like each line to finish; **(2)** in order to simulate typing the last letter of the first line press once on the space bar; **(3)** now, from this point, for the first line of your address spell it out to yourself including the spaces between the words and at the same time, back space with the back-space key, once for every single letter and space; **(4)** the point at which you stop will be the starting place for the first line of your address. Now type it; **(5)** when you get to the end of this first line, do not move your typing point, but turn up (manually) your page by one whole line; **(6)** repeat the process for the second line of your address, again spelling out this line letter by letter and back spacing at the same time. Wherever you stop will be the starting point for this second line, and so on (this method avoids having to count the letters in each line and then counting back from the right hand margin the relevant number of times. Errors are easily made that way. The point at which you finish spelling out this second line is the starting point for typing it. Almost as if by magic it should finish in perfect alignment with the line above it); **(7)** Repeat this process for each line in the address and if you wish for the date as well.

You don't need to count, measure, pray or make a wish – it should work each time. As long as you back space once for every single letter, space and comma in that line, the point at which you bring the typing point to is the starting point of that very line. What else can you use this method of line alignment for?

Name and title lists:

```
    Brian Dover    ...      ...      ...    Bishop

 Linda Brownings   ...      ...      ...    Maid

      Jon Spott    ...      ...      ...    Farmer
```

Invoices:

```
                  £

    woodwork      3.33

    plumbing     24.50

water works       4.00

  decorating     16.75
```

Once you know how, the uses will seem endless!! You'll wonder how you ever managed without knowing.

ONE WORD, TWO HANDS

○ Type the alphabet in lower case without a comma or a space between each letter.

○ Type the alphabet in lower case again, this time with a comma and a space after each letter.

○ Now type the alphabet in upper case, without locking the shift key, and with a comma and a space after each letter.

○ After this warm-up, here are the following two-handed sentences for this session (to be typed three times each, please):

Uphill we sat on a tree seat.
A jolly beggar in my street.
My mum fed a plump zebra.
My deaf badger was jolly ill.
A raw onion extract in my milk.
We greeted my pupil in Raffeta Street.
My opinion poll was set up in July.
Polly was in my pink sweater.
Look, a devastated crater in my area.
My pink pump gadget was feared wasted.

○ Now, for the long awaited two-handed words; type them three times each.

strawberry   hottest   longest   sweetly
station   joined   hopping   shopper

○ And, finally, the short two-handed commonly used words and phrases; three times each.

the   and   then   these   when   why   it was   he had
they were   we know   our chairs   your shirt   my book

• EXAMPLE

abcdefghijklmnopqrstuvwxyz
a, b, c, d, e, f, g, h, i, j, k, l, m,
n, o, p, q, r, s, t, u, v, w, x, y, z,
A, B, C, D, E, F, G, H, I, J, K, L, M,
N, O, P, Q, R, S, T, U, V, W, X, Y, Z,

Uphill we sat on a tree seat.
Uphill we sat on a tree seat.
Uphill we sat on a tree seat.

A jolly beggar in my street.
A jolly beggar in my street.
A jolly beggar in my street.

My mum fed a plump zebra.
My mum fed a plump zebra.
My mum fed a plump zebra.

My deaf badger was jolly ill.
My deaf badger was jolly ill.
My deaf badger was jolly ill.

A raw onion extract in my milk.
A raw onion extract in my milk.
A raw onion extract in my milk.

We greeted my pupil in Raffeta Street.
We greeted my pupil in Raffeta Street.
We greeted my pupil in Raffeta Street.

My opinion poll was set up in July.
My opinion poll was set up in July.
My opinion poll was set up in July.

Polly was in my pink sweater.
Polly was in my pink sweater.
Polly was in my pink sweater.

Look, a devastated crater in my area.
Look, a devastated crater in my area.
Look, a devastated crater in my area.

My pink pump gadget was feared wasted.
My pink pump gadget was feared wasted.
My pink pump gadget was feared wasted.

strawberry strawberry strawberry
hottest hottest hottest
longest longest longest
sweetly sweetly sweetly
station station station
joined joined joined
hopping hopping hopping
shopper shopper shopper
the the the
and and and
then then then
these these these
when when when
why why why
it was it was it was
he had he had he had
they were they were they were
we know we know we know
our chairs our chairs our chairs
your shirt your shirt your shirt
my book my book my book

● EXPLANATION

By now you should be beginning to feel familiar with the lay-out of the keyboard. Using the left and right hand for different words is becoming a rhythmic pattern and, in addition, typing the alphabet several times at the start of each session should familiarize you with some of the less frequently used keys. But, oh, how you have longed to type those two-handed words that the professionals bash out with such ease. I think it is useful to start this transition, from single to double-handed words, by starting off with one-handed words with 'other hand endings'. In addition, all the endings are very common and frequently used by everyone. Once you have mastered these you are well on your way to speedy two-handed keyboard control. Finally, it is time to get used to typing the two-, three- and four-letter words that require both hands and crop up with great regularity within the English language. You may as well plonk them out now – after all, you have been looking forward to them – and get used to them, they won't be phased out or disposed of yet!

AT LAST KEYBOARD CONTROL

○ Type the alphabet in lower case with a comma and a space after each letter.

○ Type the alphabet with alternate letters in upper and lower case, with a comma and a space after each letter. Be careful not to lock the shift key so that you end up with all the letters in upper case.

○ Type the following short phrases three times each:

A bat was in the rafter.

The mill was high up the hill.

We fed a fat cave bat on milk.

He had vacated his house.

She has had a secret too.

If you can, sedate the zebra.

It should be here by today.

We can have our tea soon.

He waded in up to his middle.

He is an old weaver.

It is wetter here in Wales.

Hop up on to the back of the lion.

○ Now type the following short passage, slowly and carefully. Do not hurry just because it seems longer than anything else you have typed to date. Do it twice in single-line spacing.

The weather in England during the month of July can often be rather wet; if there is a lot of rainfall in July then August is often just as wet. However, in August the nights are beginning to get longer and this may cause heavy dewfall –

sometimes there are gales and at times it may seem that autumn has already begun.

● EXAMPLE

a, b, c, d, e, f, g, h, i, j, k, l, m,
n, o, p, q, r, s, t, u, v, w, x, y, z,
A, b, C, d, E, f, G, h, I, j, K, l, M,
n, O, p, Q, r, S, t, U, v, W, x, Y, z,

A bat was in the rafter.
A bat was in the rafter.
A bat was in the rafter.

The mill was high up the hill.
The mill was high up the hill.
The mill was high up the hill.

We fed a fat cave bat on milk.
We fed a fat cave bat on milk.
We fed a fat cave bat on milk.

He had vacated his house.
He had vacated his house.
He had vacated his house.

She has had a secret too.
She has had a secret too.
She has had a secret too.

If you can, sedate the zebra.
If you can, sedate the zebra.
If you can, sedate the zebra.

It should be here by today.
It should be here by today.
It should be here by today.

We can have our tea soon.
We can have our tea soon.
We can have our tea soon.

He waded in up to his middle.
He waded in up to his middle.
He waded in up to his middle.

He is an old weaver.
He is an old weaver.
He is an old weaver.

It is wetter here in Wales.
It is wetter here in Wales.
It is wetter here in Wales.

Hop up on to the back of the lion.
Hop up on to the back of the lion.
Hop up on to the back of the lion.

The weather in England during the month of July
can often be rather wet; if there is a lot of
rainfall in July then August is often just as
wet. However, in August the nights are
beginning to get longer and this may cause heavy
dewfall - sometimes there are gales and at times
it may seem that autumn has already begun.

The weather in England during the month of July
can often be rather wet; if there is a lot of
rainfall in July then August is often just as
wet. However, in August the nights are
beginning to get longer and this may cause heavy
dewfall - sometimes there are gales and at times
it may seem that autumn has already begun.

● EXPLANATION

Using the shift key still takes some thinking about but, don't worry, it will soon become second nature to you. Practising in this way helps you to re-learn the location of the letters of the alphabet and also to use both shift keys with equal ease. The short phrases should help you to get into the swing of two-handed words, commas and the full stop with the obligatory two spaces after it every time. The short, cheery little paragraph about August weather will at least make you aware of just how many skills you now have and what those skills can do for you. Pay careful attention to the spacing after punctuation. Some of the letter combinations and also words will be familiar to you from previous exercises which should be encouraging if nothing else.

Don't try to type too fast, it will be a while yet before you can sound like a professional keyboard controller and after all it is the finished article that counts – not what you sound like while you are preparing it! So persist and persuade those fingers into the right places, think digital control and, with practice and time, speed will be acquired without a great deal of effort.

MORE KEYBOARD CONTROL

○ Warm up with your alphabet and number exercise. Don't forget the comma and space after each character.

○ Type the alphabet with alternate letters in upper and lower case. Do it twice, the first time with A as an upper-case letter, the second time as a lower-case letter.

○ Now type the following passage in double-line spacing.

Home decoration is fast becoming a hobby for many people. Today there are numerous books on the subject, covering methods and tips for the DIY enthusiasts, but you may be the sort of person that finds the initial difficulty is in deciding on the colour scheme for a room. Why not 'borrow' ideas from the professionals – look at carpets, fabrics and wallpapers – somewhere among these 3 forms you may acquire inspiration and a starting point for your own plans. Don't be afraid to experiment, some of the best schemes have often started life as an accident/experiment!

○ Try the following mini passage, be wary with the numbers, and do it twice in double-line spacing.

Fred's mum was convinced that she had bought 6 cans of dog food for their 2 dogs on the 10th March. However, she had forgotten to buy the 8 cans of cat food for the 4 cats!

○ Type the following days of the week and months of the year three times each:

Monday Tuesday Wednesday Thursday Friday Saturday Sunday

January February March April May June July

- EXAMPLE

a, b, c, d, e, f, g, h, i, j, k, l, m,
n, o, p, q, r, s, t, u, v, w, x, y, z,

1, 2, 3, 4, 5, 6, 7, 8, 9, 0,

A, b, C, d, E, f, G, h, I, j, K, l, M,
n, O, p, Q, r, S, t, U, v, W, x, Y, z,

a, B, c, D, e, F, g, H, i, J, k, L, m,
N, o, P, q, R, s, T, u, V, w, X, y, Z,

Home decoration is fast becoming a hobby for

many people. Today there are numerous books on

the subject, covering methods and tips for the

DIY enthusiasts, but you may be the sort of

person that finds the initial difficulty is in

deciding on the colour scheme for a room. Why

not 'borrow' ideas from the professionals -

look at carpets, fabrics and wallpapers -

somewhere amongst these 3 forms you may acquire

inspiration and a starting point for your own

plans. Don't be afraid to experiment, some of

the best schemes have often started life as an

accident/experiment!

Fred's mum was convinced that she had bought 6 cans of dog food for their 2 dogs on the 10th March. However, she had forgotten to buy the 8 cans of cat food for the 4 cats!

Fred's mum was convinced that she had bought 6 cans of dog food for their 2 dogs on the 10th March. However, she had forgotten to buy the 8 cans of cat food for the 4 cats!

Monday Monday Monday
Tuesday Tuesday Tuesday
Wednesday Wednesday Wednesday
Thursday Thursday Thursday
Friday Friday Friday
Saturday Saturday Saturday
Sunday Sunday Sunday

January January January
February February February
March March March

April April April
May May May
June June June

July July July
August August August
September September September

October October October
November November November
December December December

● EXPLANATION

The keyboard should now be starting to feel more and more familiar to you and you should now be able to put your fingers automatically over the right keys when you are running through the alphabet, whether in upper or lower case. This start to each session just serves to remind you where those letters are that you don't type very often and to speed up your ability to engage the shift key, to insert a comma or a space.

The passage on home decoration is purely for practice of the skills you have now acquired. Gone are the days of left and right hand words and phrases. Everything is now just as it will be. Both hands working together and, more importantly, knowing what the other is doing!

Typing the passage out in double-line spacing will help you to spot your mistakes should you make any! When, later, you have seen where they occur, just type these particular words a couple of times over to get the feel of them. Then repeat the entire passage and hopefully, you should make fewer errors this time. Don't fret if that is not the case with you just yet; it will be.

It is a good idea to get into the habit of having to type figures within your typing work. This will help to familiarize you with having to hop up to the top row of keys and the more often you do it the less it will feel strange or result in errors. It is a sensible exercise to become proficient at typing the days of the week and months of the year; again, this will help you to become better acquainted with the keyboard, the shift keys and using the comma key and the space bar without having to think about it. The greater the regularity of use, the greater the increase of keyboard control and the nearer you come to doing these functions automatically.

SESSION TEN •
CONGRATULATIONS

o   Type the alphabet in upper case throughout with a comma
    and a space after each letter.

o   Type your name and address, as if on an envelope, then
    your date of birth.

o   Type the following passage in double-line spacing (don't
    attempt a speed record yet). Be certain that you are actu-
    ally doing it correctly, rather than just hoping to:

**How to throw a pot – first you need a fair sized lump of
moist clay, which you mould by hand into a rough ball
shape. Fling it down firmly onto the wheel, as close to the
centre as is possible and then splash it with luke warm
water. Moisten your own hands and then start the wheel
turning (not too fast), now with both hands take a firm grip
of the lump and try to stop it wobbling from side to side by
forcing it into a new, perfectly balanced shape. It is now
'centred' and ready for you to turn it into a pot!!**

**Squeeze it gently and its shape will change, moderate your
grip on it and again it will change shape. Force your thumbs
down into the middle and an opening will form, pull out
gently and the rudiments of a pot will take shape in front of
you.**

o   Type the following short note (and don't forget to aim for
    accuracy rather than speed – speed won't show on the
    paper at the end of the session, but your hasty mistakes
    will!!) Type it in double-line spacing, as many times as you
    feel like – the option is now yours as a keyboard controller.

Mr Milkman, Just to let you know that on Monday you delivered 12 pints, on Tuesday you left 11 pints, and on Wednesday just 7 pints. On Thursday you kindly left me 23 pints of milk and 4 cartons of cream and the same again on Friday, with the addition of 7 loaves of brown and 10 of white bread. You'll be pleased to know that we are going away for the weekend!!

● EXAMPLE

A, B, C, D, E, F, G, H, I, J, K, L, M,
N, O, P, Q, R, S, T, U, V, W, X, Y, Z,

Mr Thomas Typist
15 Browning Avenue
Hightown
Middleshire
MD4 8SS

30 March 1965

How to throw a pot - first you need a fair sized

lump of moist clay, which you mould by hand into

a rough ball shape. Fling it down firmly onto

the wheel, as close to the centre as is possible

and then splash it with luke warm water.

Moisten your own hands and then start the wheel

turning (not too fast), now with both hands take

a firm grip of the lump and try to stop it

wobbling from side to side by forcing it into a

new, perfectly balanced shape. It is now 'centred' and ready for you to turn it into a pot!!

Squeeze it gently and its shape will change, moderate your grip on it and again it will change shape. Force your thumbs down into the middle and an opening will form, pull out gently and the rudiments of a pot will take shape in front of you.

Mr Milkman, Just to let you know that on Monday you delivered 12 pints, on Tuesday you left 11 pints, and on Wednesday just 7 pints. On Thursday you kindly left me 23 pints of milk and 4 cartons of cream and the same again on Friday, with the addition of 7 loaves of brown and 10 of white bread. You'll be pleased to know that we are going away for the weekend!!

● EXPLANATION

Well, how do you feel – that was your last lesson in this book. Ten sessions in two weeks; two-handed typing at a moderate speed, with potential for greater things. Can't be a bad start. You should feel proud of yourself and congratulations are deserved all round. I send mine to you with this closing section.

The alphabet is getting easier all the time – just like when you were learning to recite it – do you remember? Well, you've mastered the art of keyboard control as well as something else to whet your 'skills appetite' – a spot of info on pot throwing. Not forgetting the numbers on your keyboard – a quick bash at a note to the milkman.

Check over your typing for mistakes, see where they occur and try to work out why they happened, repeat the words/ phrases a couple of times or so, just to iron out any particular problem. In addition, don't be afraid to check over things that you feel unsure about, go back to a previous session if you feel the need, or just to practise a particular technique. This is the only way you will improve – if you want to.

INFORMATION SECTION
(Not essential reading for the sessions)

• AN AFTERTHOUGHT TO PONDER

I've done my best to make the rules simple and logical – the rest is up to you. The lessons are optional, but without them the rules won't stick in your mind.

o   Practice makes perfect (nearly) so keep at it.

o   Five minutes each day is better than half an hour once a week (a rule that can be applied to many things in life).

o   If it helps, keep a note of your progress – on some of the more disappointing days this may prove to be inspiring.

At the end of this book is a speed test. It is only for fun, so don't fret or worry about it. You may also find that anxiety increases your rate of mistakes and slows you down. Trembling hands are the last thing a keyboard controller wants.

o   Take it easy, don't be too hard on yourself, mistakes may one day be the only way of telling a machine from a person. Therefore, be proud of your human foibles.

• HOW DO I KNOW IF I'VE GOT PICA OR ELITE?

This is simple to work out. Type twelve characters in a continuous line. Now with a ruler, measure the length of the twelve characters. If it is precisely one inch (2.5 cms) then your typeface is 'Elite'. If, however, it is more than one inch, it is 'Pica' which means that there will be ten characters to the inch.

```
abcdefghijkl          abcdefghij

  'ELITE'               'PICA'

12 characters         10 characters

per inch              per inch
```

However, no matter which typeface your typewriter is fitted with (some electronics have the facility for both pica and elite type) there are always six lines of type (in single-line spacing) within a depth of one inch.

So, should the need ever arise, it is possible to measure out an area of one square inch or two-and-a-half square centimetres, without the use of a ruler, as follows:

```
OXOXOXOXOXOX          XOXOXOXOXO
XOXOXOXOXOXO          OXOXOXOXOX
OXOXOXOXOXOX          XOXOXOXOXO
XOXOXOXOXOXO          OXOXOXOXOX
OXOXOXOXOXOX          XOXOXOXOXO
XOXOXOXOXOXO          OXOXOXOXOX

AN ELITE              A PICA
SQUARE INCH.          SQUARE INCH
```

If you are fully metricated, you will find that there are five character spaces to the centimetre in Elite type and four in Pica type. However, the typewriter is fundamentally old-fashioned; after all, it was invented in Britain long before the British became metric and typefaces are still gauged in inches rather than centimetres.

• SOME INTERESTING FACTS AND FIGURES

A4: The most common size of typing paper is the international standard size, A4. When you insert it into a typewriter, some interesting things can be noted. It's not essential information, just intriguing.

A4 is 210mm × 297mm and if your typeface is Elite, this means that there are 100 character spaces across the page and seventy lines in depth if the paper is inserted 'portrait' wise, i.e. the shorter edge is horizontal. The exact centre of your portrait page will be thirty-five lines down and fifty character spaces in from the left hand edge.

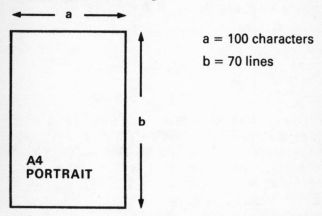

a = 100 characters
b = 70 lines

A4
PORTRAIT

If the paper is inserted 'landscape', i.e. the longest edge is horizontal of the page, then there are 140 characters across the page and fifty lines in depth. The exact centre of the landscape page will be twenty-five lines down from the top of the page and seventy spaces in from the left hand edge.

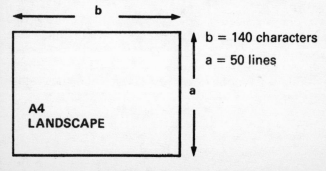

b = 140 characters
a = 50 lines

A4
LANDSCAPE

A5 is exactly half the size of A4 paper, that is 148mm × 210mm. This means that there are seventy character spaces across the page and fifty lines in depth if the paper is inserted portrait wise. The exact centre of the A5 portrait page will be twenty-five lines down from the top edge of the page and thirty-five characters in from the left-hand edge.

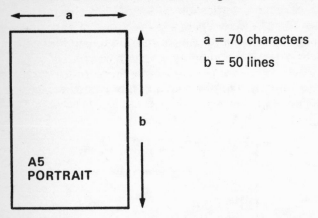

a = 70 characters

b = 50 lines

If the paper is inserted landscape, there are 100 characters across the page and thirty-five lines in depth. The exact centre of the A5 landscape page is seventeen-and-a-half lines down from the top edge of the page and fifty character spaces in from the left-hand edge.

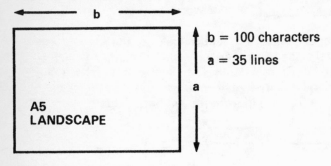

b = 100 characters

a = 35 lines

● CROSSWORDS

Given the information we now have about the number of lines and characters on an A4 and A5 page, it is simple to deduce that each line of type on the horizontal plane takes up two character spaces on the vertical plane. In addition, this means that there are two character spaces to the depth of each line. This is not 'essential keyboard control information' unless you just happen to wish to type up your own crossword.

Bear in mind that all 'across' words must be typed with a space after each letter and all 'down' words are to be typed in single-line spacing and your crossword should appear as follows:

```
P I L L A R
U       I   A
P   F L A M E
P L A Y   B
E   V     L
T R O U P E R
    U     R
    R
```

On the other hand, if you would like your crossword to appear in double-line spacing then you will need to leave three spaces after each letter of the 'across' words.

```
P   I   L   L   A   R

U           I   A

P       F   L   A   M   E

P   L   A   Y       B

E       V           L

T   R   O   U   P   E   R

        U           R

        R
```

• COMBINATION CHARACTERS

Some typewriters have a multitude of characters and your needs seem never to exhaust the variations open to you. However, some typewriters have just the bare essentials and with a little know-how and a jot of imagination it is possible to acquire more characters. They are known as 'combination characters' because you type two characters, one on top of the other in a single character space.

These are some of the possibilities, followed by their name and instructions on how to make them. Note that bs stands for back space.

!	Exclamation mark	*Apostrophe, back space (bs), full stop.*
✱	Asterisk	*Lower case x, bs, dash.*
÷	Division sign	*Colon, bs, dash.*
⌷	Dollar sign	*Capital S, bs, solidus (slant sign).*
'	Feet or minutes	*Apostrophe sign.*
"	Inches or seconds or umlaut	*Quotation sign.*
–	Minus	*Dash (hyphen) sign.*
x	Multiplication sign	*Lower case x.*
‡	Dagger	*Exclamation mark, bs, dash.*
(c)	Copyright sign	*Bracket, lower case c, bracket.*
§ §	Section sign	*Upper case S, move the paper up a fraction, repeat upper case S. (It may be done in lower case also.)*
/ (	Opening square bracket	*Solidus, bs, turn up half a line, dash, turn down one line, dash, turn up half a line to realign.*

94

⌐]	Closing square bracket	*Solidus, bs 2, turn up half a line, dash, turn the paper down a single line, dash, turn up half a line to realign.*
⋇	Large asterisk	*Upper case X, bs, dash.*
=	Equals sign	*Dash, bs, turn up a fraction dash, realign.*

• COMPLICATED COMBINATIONS

You may never use these characters, but if the need should ever arise, the method to be employed is outlined here for reference.

This may be used as a border for presentation work. Type the figure '8', back space, turn up half a line and repeat the '8' character. Do this until you have the required length of vertical line. To type similar horizontal lines you will need to turn your paper round and replace it in the typewriter.

Again, this is a border edge. Type the figure '8', turn up half a line, bs, then type a full stop, turn up by a single line, type '8' and repeat from the beginning until you have the required length of line. Turn the paper around to type horizontal lines.

Wavy brackets, or also a border edge. Type an open bracket, bs, turn up half a line, type a closed bracket, bs, turn up half a line, open bracket, bs, turn up a half line and continue for desired length of bracket. Always start and finish on a single bracket at the top and bottom of the wavy line.

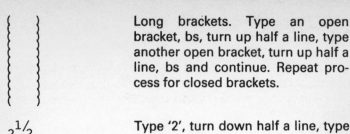

Long brackets. Type an open bracket, bs, turn up half a line, type another open bracket, turn up half a line, bs and continue. Repeat process for closed brackets.

$2\frac{1}{2}$

Type '2', turn down half a line, type '1/' then turn up half a line, bs just half a space, then type '2'.

(If your electronic machine has no facility for back spacing by half a space, then move forward half a space, then back space a single space. On an old manual, back space a whole space, then depress the space bar – this will move the typing point forward half a space – do not release it until you have typed in the last character in the fraction.)

$10\frac{13}{16}$ths.

Type '10', turn down the paper half a line, type '13/' then turn up half a line, bs half a space, then type '16ths'.

● TYPING NUMBERS

Sometimes there seems to be a bit of confusion about how to type numbers; do you type the numbers as words, can you type numbers as weights and measures in an abbreviated form, or what?

The answer is to be consistent and these are the ways in which you can be:

○ **One metre ten centimetres**
○ **1 metre 10 centimetres**
○ **1m 10cm**
○ **110cm**

All these forms are correct, the only thing you have to ensure is that you use the same method throughout your text.

○ **Two feet nine inches**
○ **2 feet 9 inches**
○ **2ft 9ins**
○ **2' 9"**

Again all these forms are correct. Note that the abbreviated words are typed immediately after the numbers. Likewise the single and double quotation marks.

○ **Four minutes six seconds**
○ **4 minutes 6 seconds**
○ **4mins 6secs**
○ **4' 6"**

Any other variations from these or any mixtures of these forms are not correct. Be careful not to mix figures with the word version of a number.

○ **Ten and a half years old.**
○ **10½ years old.**
○ **10½ yrs.**

Be consistent. If within a text you have numbers for various sizes, ages, weights etc., type them either as all words, or all figures, either with abbreviations throughout or not at all. Do not swap from one style to another and back again.

• HOW TO TYPE A FORM THE DOTTY WAY

Typing forms can be a nasty and time-consuming piece of work; the easiest way to deal with them is the dotty way.

Everything is typed in upper case, followed by two spaces and the rest of the line is full stops; just dots. Each row of dots should end at the same 'spot'. Type in double-line spacing and this will allow sufficient room for a keyboard controller to fill in the completed form.

NAME ....

ADDRESS ....

OCCUPATION ....

QUALIFICATIONS ....

....

....

HOW USEFUL HAVE YOU FOUND THIS COURSE ....

....

WOULD YOU RECOMMEND IT TO OTHERS ....

DID YOU MANAGE TO COMPLETE IT, IF NOT WHY NOT

....

....

....

Filling in the form there are two points to remember:

   (1) type just above the dotted line; and

   (2) form a common starting point for each line so that the filled-in answers create a large margin of their own. (If there are longer questions on the form, start a second/alternative starting point specifically for these lines.)

This is the form from the previous page, partially filled in:

```
                    Thomas Typist
NAME      .........................................

                    55 The Avenue
ADDRESS   .......................................

                    Uptown, Dampshire
.................................................

                    Salesman
OCCUPATION  .....................................
```

Personally, I don't think it is necessary to put a question mark in after every question on a form – you can't type in a full stop, therefore it is merely being consistent.

o   Never type a form in single-line spacing, as this will not leave enough room to fill in the answers.

o   Yes/no answers should be deleted with a lower case x.

• HANDY HINTS FROM AN OLD HAND

Cleaning the typeface	Use a blob of 'Blu-Tack' or a similar material and press into each of the letters several times to remove excess ink which clogs the letters and creates a blobby appearance.
Extracting dust	Use a slightly damp small artist's brush or lipstick brush and poke gently into the fluffy crevices.
Tricky bits	Spill a small quantity of methylated spirits on to the dirty and inaccessible parts – this will drain the dirt away on to the table or newspaper placed underneath the typewriter and will leave the typewriter parts dry almost immediately.
Cleaning the outside	Use a household cleaning spray and a soft cloth.
Cleaning the platen	Use a blob of cotton wool dampened with methylated spirits.
Between the keys	Use the damp corner of a duster, or use a soft-headed brush on your vacuum-cleaner nozzle.
Storing	Always store your typewriter/keyboard with a dust cover on. You'd be surprised at the amount of dust and dirt that finds your typewriter a perfect new home.

Avoid platen damage

Type with two sheets of paper in your machine; this reduces the 'noise' of typing and also reduces the intensity of the pounding of the keys on your platen.

● A FUN SPEED TEST

Note that this is not to be taken seriously, it just gives you an idea of how you have progressed over the last few days. Type the following passage in double-line spacing. Ask someone to time your typing for precisely one minute. At the end of that period of time you must stop typing. Whatever point you have got to will be an indicator of your typing speed (in words per minute) and do not forget to deduct one word for every single mistake!! So if you type cautiously, you will probably end up with a faster overall typing speed than if you race along reck-lessly.

If you finish the passage in exactly one minute you have a typing speed of exactly eighty-two words per minute! How-ever, a reasonable speed at this stage would be between twenty and thirty words per minute. Soon though, you will be faster than that, especially if you have access to a keyboard on a regular basis.

For thousands of years people have enjoyed making	10 wds
and drinking wine. It is a time-consuming process	20 wds
but well worth it in the end. Today modern tech-	30 wds
nology has enabled scientists to develop wine-making	40 wds
methods that take only a matter of weeks. Kits	50 wds
bought in the morning can be fermenting away by	60 wds
late afternoon, and three weeks later bottled and	70 wds
stored or drunk immediately in the comfort of your	80 wds
own home.	82 wds

Each completed line is ten words (five characters and/or spaces is the equivalent of one word) and therefore two lines in a minute would give you a keyboard speed of twenty words per minute.

GLOSSARY

Automatic corrector: this is another term for the self-correcting function. First you need to have noticed your mistake and then you engage a special key; this is a reversing key and, while you hold it down, the typing point moves in reverse, at the same time, engaging the lift-off tape and removing all the letters you have typed, until you release the key. It is possible to remove several lines of type – depending on the size of your keyboard's memory. Alternatively, a quick press on the key will remove only the last character typed.

Buffer key: some electronic typewriters have a small memory, so that when your typing point is returning to the start of a new line, it is possible to continue typing during this returning process – the 'buffer' memory 'stores' the keys you have depressed. Up to thirty characters may be stored in it.

Correctable ribbon: this is a carbon-covered band specifically designed for electronic typewriters. It can be used only once but has the advantage of enabling invisible corrections to be made with the aid of 'lift-off tapes'.

Correcting fluid/liquid: see *Tipp-Ex*.

Daisywheel:	this is a piece of plastic, approximately eight centimetres in diameter, shaped rather like a daisy. At the end of each 'petal' is a character. The advantage of the daisywheel is that it allows you to change your typeface to any other available style; currently there are about a dozen different typefaces.
Dual/multiple pitch:	a typewriter with this facility is capable of typing in either 10, 12, or 15 pitch (characters per inch). Some typewriters possess a 'proportional spacing' function in addition to the three pitches.
Electric/electronic:	the electric preceded the electronic typewriter. It is possible to type much faster on an electric typewriter than on a manual, but it does not possess any of the modern functions found on an electronic machine, e.g. self-correction, choice of pitch, buffer memory or interchangeable typeface.
Golf ball:	these are metal components, again specifically made for electric/electronic typewriters, shaped like small golfballs. On the surface of the ball are the typeface characters. Golfballs are sturdier than daisywheels, but much more expensive. *Note*: it is not possible to swop from a daisywheel to a golfball on an electronic typewriter, as individual machines are designed for exclusive use with either daisywheel or golfball.
Impression selector:	there is normally a button on most typewriters that enables you to choose how hard or softly you will

have to hit the keys in order to get them to work.

Justified margin: all typewriters and keyboards are capable of forming justified left-hand margins, where every line of type starts at exactly the same point, at the left-hand edge. Electronic typewriters and word-processors with this function can often perform this task with the right-hand edge of the typed work. The text is typed into the machine as you wish it to be displayed, then the machine retypes it with a justified right-hand margin, giving the work the appearance of a printed book page.

Lift-off tape: otherwise known as self-correcting tape. Again this is a feature of the electronic typewriter. In effect it is a narrow strip of sticky tape that once engaged lifts off the ink of the incorrect character(s) from the typed page. Mistakes then become an ink-free indentation on the paper.

NCR Paper: no carbon required paper. Forms are often printed on this type of paper, as it does not require the use of carbon paper between the sheets in order to make duplicates. The ink is contained in the backing surface of the paper and is released when impacted by a character from a typewriter or the pressure of handwriting.

Proportional spacing: this is a facility on some electric and some electronic typewriters whereby the space left between each letter is regulated automatically according to the letter typed and more specifically according to the width of the character. For instance, a lower-case letter 'i' is a narrow letter and, therefore, does not require as much space as say the letter 'm'. The overall effect of this function is that the typed text looks like book print, but the drawback comes when trying to insert/substitute a wide letter in a narrow letter's space! Corrections look obvious.

Relocating function: this key enables you to stop typing, go back to an error elsewhere on the page, correct it, and then by depressing the relocation key, go straight back to the point where you had stopped your typing prior to making the correction.

Repeating function: this key, normally located to the left of the space bar will repeat any key that has been depressed immediately before it, including carriage return, space bar or automatic-correction key, as well as all the characters on the keyboard.

Ribbon cassette: this is another term for correctable ribbons, but also includes ink ribbons for electronic typewriters. They drop and slot into electronic machines very easily and have the appearance of an audio cassette.

Typeface: this is the shape and size of your characters on your keyboard. There are many varieties to suit most tastes, including a script typeface which gives the appearance of neatly handwritten work!

Tipp-Ex: the brand name of a correcting fluid that has now become a familiar term to describe all such correcting liquids. The white fluid is painted over typing errors with the aid of a small brush provided within the bottle and secured to the top. Today correcting fluids come in a variety of colours to match the paper you are typing on.

Tipp-Ex paper: this is a small strip of paper with a thin dry coating of Tipp-Ex on the reverse side which when typed over an error will conceal the mistake that had been made.

Typing style: this is the personal preference of the keyboard controller and can be modern (open punctuation with blocked paragraphs) or classic (full punctuation with indented paragraphs) – or a variation thereof!

Typing pitch selector: if you have an electronic typewriter with a choice of typing pitch, e.g. 10 pitch (Pica) or 12 pitch (Elite) then in order to make the choice, you move a button to your preferred typing pitch. Be careful to make sure it is compatible with your daisywheel or golfball otherwise you will create some interesting hybrid typefaces. But feel free to experiment!

FOR THE BEST IN PAPERBACKS, LOOK FOR THE 🐧

In every corner of the world, on every subject under the sun, Penguin represents quality and variety – the very best in publishing today.

For complete information about books available from Penguin – including Pelicans, Puffins, Peregrines and Penguin Classics – and how to order them, write to us at the appropriate address below. Please note that for copyright reasons the selection of books varies from country to country.

In the United Kingdom: Please write to *Dept E.P., Penguin Books Ltd, Harmondsworth, Middlesex, UB7 0DA*

If you have any difficulty in obtaining a title, please send your order with the correct money, plus ten per cent for postage and packaging, to *PO Box No 11, West Drayton, Middlesex*

In the United States: Please write to *Dept BA, Penguin, 299 Murray Hill Parkway, East Rutherford, New Jersey 07073*

In Canada: Please write to *Penguin Books Canada Ltd, 2801 John Street, Markham, Ontario L3R 1B4*

In Australia: Please write to the *Marketing Department, Penguin Books Australia Ltd, P.O. Box 257, Ringwood, Victoria 3134*

In New Zealand: Please write to the *Marketing Department, Penguin Books (NZ) Ltd, Private Bag, Takapuna, Auckland 9*

In India: Please write to *Penguin Overseas Ltd, 706 Eros Apartments, 56 Nehru Place, New Delhi, 110019*

In Holland: Please write to *Penguin Books Nederland B.V., Postbus 195, NL–1380AD Weesp, Netherlands*

In Germany: Please write to *Penguin Books Ltd, Friedrichstrasse 10–12, D–6000 Frankfurt Main 1, Federal Republic of Germany*

In Spain: Please write to *Longman Penguin España, Calle San Nicolas 15, E–28013 Madrid, Spain*

In France: Please write to *Penguin Books Ltd, 39 Rue de Montmorency, F-75003, Paris, France*

In Japan: Please write to *Longman Penguin Japan Co Ltd, Yamaguchi Building, 2–12–9 Kanda Jimbocho, Chiyoda-Ku, Tokyo 101, Japan*

FOR THE BEST IN PAPERBACKS, LOOK FOR THE

PENGUIN REFERENCE BOOKS

The Penguin English Dictionary

Over 1,000 pages long and with over 68,000 definitions, this cheap, compact and totally up-to-date book is ideal for today's needs. It includes many technical and colloquial terms, guides to pronunciation and common abbreviations.

The Penguin Reference Dictionary

The ideal comprehensive guide to written and spoken English the world over, with detailed etymologies and a wide selection of colloquial and idiomatic usage. There are over 100,000 entries and thousands of examples of how words are actually used – all clear, precise and up-to-date.

The Penguin English Thesaurus

This unique volume will increase anyone's command of the English language and build up your word power. Fully cross-referenced, it includes synonyms of every kind (formal or colloquial, idiomatic and figurative) for almost 900 headings. It is a must for writers and utterly fascinating for any English speaker.

The Penguin Dictionary of Quotations

A treasure-trove of over 12,000 new gems and old favourites, from Aesop and Matthew Arnold to Xenophon and Zola.

FOR THE BEST IN PAPERBACKS, LOOK FOR THE

PENGUIN REFERENCE BOOKS

The Penguin Guide to the Law

This acclaimed reference book is designed for everyday use, and forms the most comprehensive handbook ever published on the law as it affects the individual.

The Penguin Medical Encyclopedia

Covers the body and mind in sickness and in health, including drugs, surgery, history, institutions, medical vocabulary and many other aspects. 'Highly commendable' – *Journal of the Institute of Health Education*

The Penguin French Dictionary

This invaluable French-English, English-French dictionary includes both the literary and dated vocabulary needed by students, and the up-to-date slang and specialized vocabulary (scientific, legal, sporting, etc) needed in everyday life. As a passport to the French language, it is second to none.

A Dictionary of Literary Terms

Defines over 2,000 literary terms (including lesser known, foreign language and technical terms) explained with illustrations from literature past and present.

The Penguin Map of Europe

Covers all land eastwards to the Urals, southwards to North Africa and up to Syria, Iraq and Iran. Scale – 1:5,500,000, 4-colour artwork. Features main roads, railways, oil and gas pipelines, plus extra information including national flags, currencies and populations.

The Penguin Dictionary of Troublesome Words

A witty, straightforward guide to the pitfalls and hotly disputed issues in standard written English, illustrated with examples and including a glossary of grammatical terms and an appendix on punctuation.

FOR THE BEST IN PAPERBACKS, LOOK FOR THE

PENGUIN SELF-STARTERS

Self-Starters is a new series designed to help you develop skills and proficiency in the subject of your choice. Each book has been written by an expert and is suitable for school-leavers, students, those considering changing their career in mid-stream and all those who study at home.

Titles published or in preparation:

Accounting	Noel Trimming
Advertising	Michael Pollard
Basic Statistics	Peter Gwilliam
A Career in Banking	Sheila Black, John Brennan
Clear English	Vivian Summers
French	Anne Stevens
German	Anna Nyburg
Good Business Communication	Doris Wheatley
Marketing	Marsaili Cameron, Angela Rushton, David Carson
Nursing	David White
Personnel Management	J. D. Preston
Public Relations	Sheila Black, John Brennan
Public Speaking	Vivian Summers
Retailing	David Couch
Secretarial Skills	Gale Cornish, Charlotte Coudrille, Joan Lipkin-Edwardes
Starting a Business on a Shoestring	Michel Syrett, Chris Dunn
Understanding Data	Peter Sprent